GLAMOUR KNITS
AT HOME

Glamour
Knits
AT HOME

15 sensuous designs to knit and keep forever

ERIKA KNIGHT
COLLECTIBLES

photography by Katya de Grunwald

POTTER
CRAFT

New York

Editorial director Jane O'Shea
Creative director Helen Lewis
Designer Claire Peters
Project editor Lisa Pendreigh
Editorial assistant Andrew Bayliss
Pattern checker Rosy Tucker
Photographer Katya de Grunwald
Photographer's assistant Amy Gwatkin
Stylist Beth Dadswell
Illustrator Bridget Bodoano
Pattern illustrator Anthony Duke
Production director Vincent Smith
Production controller Bridget Fish

www.crownpublishing.com
www.pottercraft.com

POTTER CRAFT and
CLARKSON N. POTTER
are trademarks and
POTTER and colophon are registered
trademarks of Random House, Inc.

Originally published in Great Britain by
Quadrille Publishing Limited, London.

Library of Congress Cataloging-in-Publication
Data is available.

ISBN-13: 978-0-307-39470-5
ISBN-10: 0-307-39470-0

Printed and bound in China

10 9 8 7 6 5 4 3 2 1

First Potter Craft Edition

introduction

Glamour Knits at Home is a decorative collection of knitted pieces designed to add a little extravagance to everyday interiors. Each design is created with decadence in mind, from sumptuous cushions in silk, satin-like cotton, delicate mohair, or ornate jacquard to a vintage-inspired throw with Oriental patterning and knitted lace; as well as a whimsical tea-cozy, silver sequinned lampshade, and rose-scented sachets. The yarns are sensuous, soft, and pretty, in a palette of pearl pink, antique rose, amethyst, Tiffany blue, petticoat peach, soft gold, and lacquer black. The stitches are simple, yet lavishly married with sumptuous fabrics, prints, and patterns, and the little details add further surprise and more than a touch of luxury with ribbons, tassels, beads, sequins, and petite bows.

glamour knits at home collection

The pattern for the round ruched cushion begins on page 42.

The pattern for the boudoir lampshade begins on page 46.

The pattern for the jacquard bolster begins on page 50.

The pattern for the pooch cushion begins on page 56.

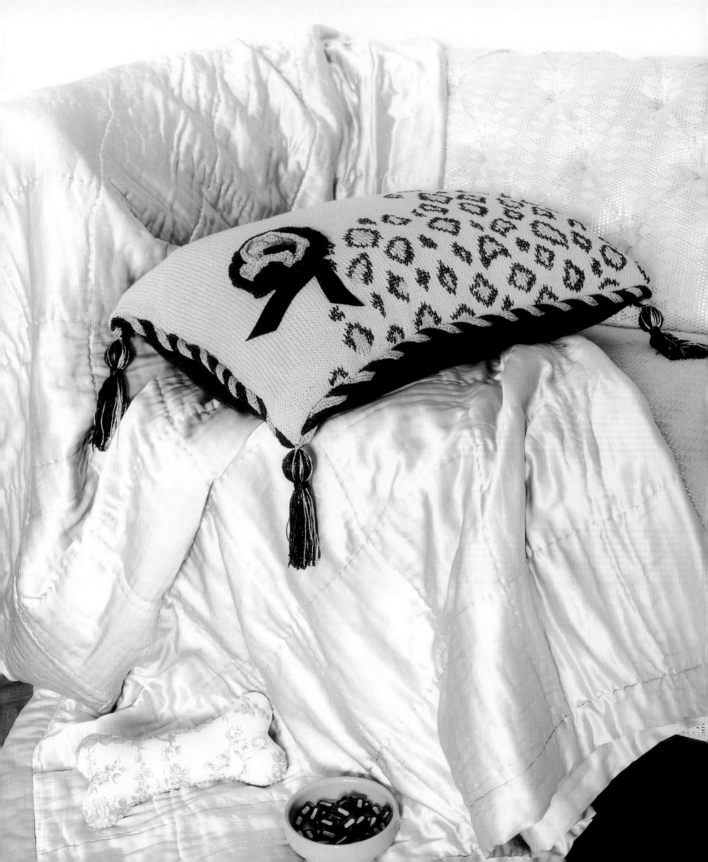

The pattern for the ornate slippers begins on page 62.

The pattern for the pleated ruffle cushion begins on page 66.

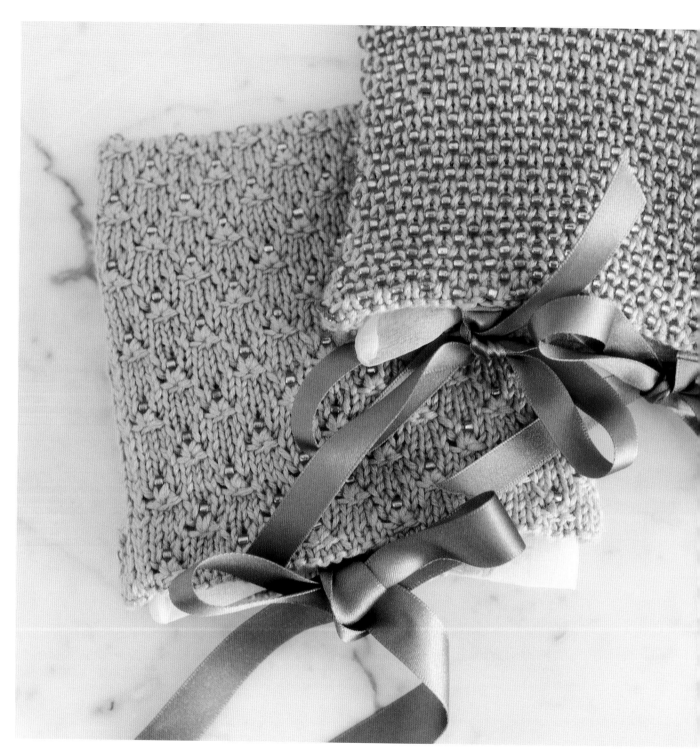

The patterns for the scented squares begin on page 70.

The pattern for the chinoiserie throw begins on page 74.

The pattern for the boudoir cushion begins on page 78.

The pattern for the tea party tea-cozy begins on page 82.

The pattern for the jacquard cushion begins on page 84.

The pattern for the dress hanger begins on page 88.

The pattern for the knot stitch cushion begins on page 92.

The pattern for the key fob begins on page 94.

The patterns for the pearl button and lace sequin cushions begin on page 98.

the
patterns

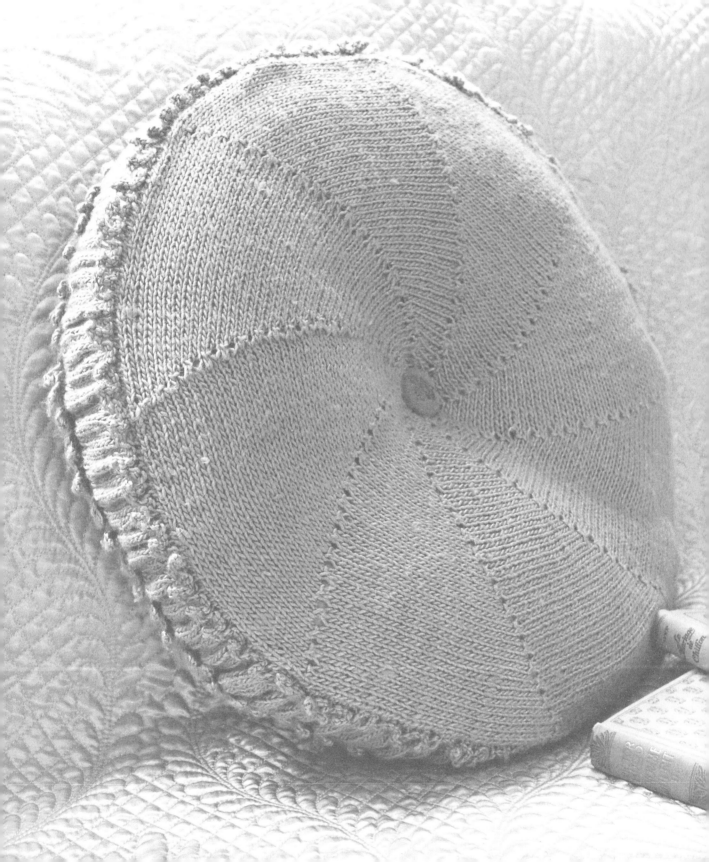

round ruched cushion

Made in a pure silk yarn in the prettiest of soft greens, this cushion is a beautiful accessory for any couch or bed. The round cushion shape is achieved using easy short-row shapings, which are simple but effective. The border is worked in a ruched stitch edged with little picots, while the front and back are both finished with a covered button that enhances the cushion's vintage character.

See pages 10–11

materials

Any double-knitting-weight yarn, such as Debbie Bliss *Pure Silk*
 Four 1¾ oz (50g) hanks
Pair of size 6 (4mm) knitting needles
Size 5 (3.75mm) circular knitting needle
Large blunt-ended yarn needle
Pins
16 in (40cm) round pillow form with gusset
2 large 1¼ in (30mm) cover buttons
Scrap of green silk fabric or ribbon to cover buttons

size

One size, approximately 16 in (40cm) in diameter

gauge

24 sts and 32 rows = 4 in (10cm) over St st using size 6 (4mm)
 needles or size necessary to obtain gauge.

pattern notes

• For the short-row shaping, when the instructions say "turn" at the
 end of the row, this means that the remaining stitches are not
 worked. To avoid creating a hole when turning on a knit row, work
 a wrap stitch—knit as far as instructed, then slip the next stitch
 purlwise onto the right-hand needle, bring the yarn forward
 between the two needles, slip the stitch back to the left-hand
 needle and take the yarn to the back between the two needles,
 turn, and purl to the end of the next row.
• Keep precious yarns, such as silk, in a pillowcase while you work to
 avoid snagging the yarn.

To make cushion front

Using size 6 (4mm) needles, cast on 44 sts.

Work in St st and short rows as foll:

Row 1: K all sts.

Row 2: P all sts.

Row 3: K to last 2 sts, turn (see pattern notes).

Row 4: P.

Row 5: K to last 4 sts, turn.

Row 6: P.

Cont working in short rows as set, leaving 2 more sts unworked on every knit row until there are no more sts to knit.

This completes the first segment of circle.

Start again with row 1 and cont until 8 segments have been worked to form a full circle.

Do not bind off sts, but join last segment to first segment by grafting one st from needle with corresponding st on cast-on edge.

To make cushion back

Work exactly as for cushion front.

To make ruched gusset

Using size 5 (3.75mm) circular needle, work picot cast-on edging as foll:

*Cast on 6 sts onto left needle using knit-on cast-on method, bind off 3 sts, slip st left on right needle onto left needle; rep from * until 276 sts have been cast on onto left needle.

Beg with a k row, work 4 rows in St st, ending with RS facing for next row.

Next row (RS): K1, *k into front and back of next st; rep from * to last st, k1.

Beg with a p row, work 6 rows in St st, ending with WS facing for next row.

Next row (WS): P1, *p2tog; rep from * to last st, p1.

Beg with a k row, work 4 rows in St st, ending with RS facing for next row.

Work a picot bind-off edge as foll:
*Bind off 6 sts, slip st left on right needle onto left needle, cast on 3 sts; rep from * to end.

To finish

Weave in any loose yarn ends.

Lay front and back out flat and gently steam. (Do not steam ruched gusset.)

Sew together row ends of ruched gusset to form a circle.

The gusset is sewn to cushion leaving picot edgings free.

To make it easier to sew on, measure gusset, then divide into eight equal sections, and mark them with a pin. Pin each section on one side of gusset to a segment of cushion front and hand stitch gusset to front.

Hand stitch gusset to cushion back in same way, leaving an opening for inserting pillow form. Insert pillow form and hand sew opening closed. Cover buttons with silk fabric. Position one button at center of each side of cushion and sew them together, stitching through cushion and pulling thread tightly to indent center of cushion.

boudoir lampshade

Slip this opulent lacy cover over your current lampshade to add a touch of feminine glamour to a bedside table or dresser. Knitted in mercerized cotton, it is made up of six segments, three in Turkish stitch and three in diamond stitch, and has a pretty edging at the top and bottom. The finished cover is embellished with matte and shiny sequins along with glass beads for a gentle shimmer.

See pages 12–13

materials

Any super-fine-weight mercerized cotton yarn, such as
    Yeoman *Cotton Cannele 4 Ply*
    One $8^3/_4$ oz (250g) cone
Pair each of size 3 (3.25mm), 6 (4mm) and 9 (5.5mm) knitting needles
Medium-size blunt-ended yarn needle
Approximately 100 small (8mm) matte silver sequins
Approximately 20 medium (10mm) shiny silver sequins
Approximately 220 small (3mm) clear glass seed beads
Approximately 50 small (7mm) clear glass bugle beads
Sewing needle and sewing thread for sewing on beads
Lampshade, approximately $28^1/_2$ in (72cm) around lower edge,
    $14^1/_4$ in (36cm) around upper edge, and $6^3/_4$ in (17cm) tall

size

One size, approximately $6^3/_4$ in (17cm) tall

gauge

Turkish stitch: 10 sts = $2^1/_2$ in (6cm) over pattern using size 3 (4mm)
    needles or size necessary to obtain gauge.
Diamond stitch: 12 sts = $2^1/_2$ in (6cm) over pattern using size 3 (4mm)
    needles or size necessary to obtain gauge.

To make Turkish stitch panels (make 3)

With size 9 (5.5mm) needles, cast on 10 sts.

Work 2 rows in garter st (k every row).

Patt row 1: K2, *yo, sl 1, k1, psso; rep from * to last 2 sts, k2.

Rep last row 6 times more.

Next row (inc row): K into front and back of first st, k1, *yo, sl 1, k1, psso; rep from * to last 2 sts, k into front and back of next st, k1.

Cont in patt as set **and at the same time** inc 1 st as before at each end of 4 foll 6th rows—*20 sts.*

Work even in patt for 4 rows.

Work 2 rows in garter st.

Bind off knitwise.

To make diamond stitch panels (make 3)

Using size 6 (4mm) needles, cast on 11 sts.

Work 2 rows in garter st.

Row 1 (RS): P2, k2tog [k1, yo] twice, k1, sl 1, k1, psso, p2.

Row 2 and every foll WS row: K2, p7, k2.

Row 3: P2, k2tog, yo, k3, yo, sl 1, k1, psso, p2.

Row 5: P2, k1, yo, sl 1, k1, psso, k1, k2tog, yo, k1, p2.

Row 7: P2, k2, yo, sl 1, k2tog, psso, yo, k2, p2.

Row 8: Rep row 2.

Rep last 8 rows to form diamond stitch patt **and at the same time** inc 1 st at each end of next row and then at each end of every foll 4th row until there are 27 sts, taking inc sts into St st.

Cont in patt until row 8 of 5th diamond stitch patt repeat is complete.

Work 2 rows in garter st.

Bind off knitwise.

Edging

Using size 3 (3.25mm) needles, cast on 6 sts.

Row 1 (WS): K1, k2tog, yo, k2, [yo] twice, k1—*8 sts.*

Row 2: K1, [k1 tbl] twice into double yo, k2tog, yo, k3.

Row 3: K1, k2tog, yo, k5.

Row 4: Bind off 2 sts, k2tog, yo, k3—*6 sts.*

Rep last 4 rows until work fits around lower edge of shade.

Bind off.

Rep on upper edge of shade.

To finish

Weave in any loose yarn ends.

Pin out six panels and gently steam.

Lay panels side by side, alternating stitch patterns, and graft them together.

Grafting loosely to maintain lace effect, join straight edge of edgings to upper and lower edges.

Sew sequins and beads randomly to main panels and stitch beads to lower edging.

jacquard bolster

This substantial bolster cushion is made up of patchwork squares—in both lacy knit stitches and decorative fabrics. Each end of the cushion is finished with a circle knitted using a simple short-row shaping technique and is decorated with a chunky tassel and button detail.

See pages 14–15

materials

Any super-fine-weight cotton yarns, such as:

A: Small amount of Jaeger *Siena* in light dusky green

B: Small amount of Rowan *Cotton Glacé* in ocher brown

C: Small amount of Yeoman *Cotton Cannele 4 Ply* in beige

D: One 8¾ oz (250g) cone of Yeoman *Cotton Cannele 4 Ply* in brown

E: Small amount of Yeoman *Cotton Cannele 4 Ply* in gray

Approximately ⅓ yd (30cm) in each of four fabrics:

F: Chinoiserie fabric in gray/black

G: Silk fabric in green

H: Silk jacquard in gold/aqua

I: Silk dupioni in taupe

Pair of size 3 (3.25mm) knitting needles

Medium-size blunt-ended yarn needle

Bolster cushion, 18 in (45cm) long x 6¾ in (17cm) in diameter

17 large mother-of-pearl buttons, ¾ in (2cm) in diameter

24 small mother-of-pearl buttons, ½ in (1.5cm) in diameter

Microfilament sewing thread

Black fusible interfacing for backing squares

Piece of cardboard 4¾ in (12cm) by 10 in (25cm)

size

One size, approximately 18 in (45cm) long x 6¾ in (17cm) in diameter

gauge

Each knitted square measures 6 in (15cm) by 6 in (15cm) using size 3 (3.25mm) needles or size necessary to obtain gauge.

pattern note

For the short-row shaping, when the instructions say "turn" at the end of the row, this means that the remaining stitches are not worked. To avoid creating a hole when turning on a knit row, work a wrap stitch—knit as far as instructed, then slip the next stitch purlwise onto the right-hand needle, bring the yarn forward between the two needles, slip the stitch back to the left-hand needle and take the yarn to the back between the two needles, turn, and purl to the end of the next row.

special abbreviations

Cr2L = pass right needle behind first st on left needle and k 2nd st tbl, then k first st and slip both sts off left needle.

Cr2R = pass right needle in front of first st on left needle and p 2nd st, then p first st and slip both sts off left needle.

To make circular ends for bolster (make 2)

Using size 3 (3.25mm) needles and D, cast on 20 sts.

Work in garter st and short rows as foll:

Row 1: K all sts.

Row 2: K all sts.

Row 3: K to last 2 sts, turn (see pattern note).

Row 4: K.

Row 5: K to last 4 sts, turn.

Row 6: K.

Cont working in short rows as set, leaving 2 more sts unworked on every alternate knit row until there are no more sts to knit.

This completes the first segment of circle.

Start again with row 1 and cont until 12 segments have been worked to form a full circle.

Do not bind off sts, but join last segment to first segment by grafting one st from needle with corresponding st on cast-on edge.

To make tassels (make 2)

Wrap a generous amount of each color yarn used around a piece of cardboard 4¾ in (12cm) by 10 in (25cm).

Wrap a length of yarn a few times around strands at one end of cardboard and knot, leaving long enough loose ends for stitching tassel in place. Cut strands at other end of tassel (see page 97).

Wrap another length of yarn around tassel, approximately 1 in (2.5cm) from top, linking and securing ends under wrapping. Make a second tassel in same way.

Checks and cords square

Using size 3 (3.25mm) needles and C, cast on 34 sts.

Row 1 (RS): K1, *k4, p2, Cr2L,

p2; rep from * to last st, k1.
Row 2: P1, *k2, Cr2R, k2, p4; rep from * to last st, p1.
Rows 3–6: Rep rows 1 and 2 twice.
Row 7: K1, *p1, Cr2L, p2, k4, p1; rep from * to last st, k1.
Row 8: P1, *k1, p4, k2, Cr2R, k1; rep from * to last st, p1.
Rows 9–12: Rep rows 7 and 8 twice.
Rep last 12 rows until square measures 6in (15cm). Bind off.

Blackberry stitch squares (make 3)

Using size 3 (3.25mm) needles and A, cast on 34 sts.
Row 1 (RS): K1, *[k1, yo, k1] into next st, p3; rep from * to last st, k1.
Row 2: P1, *p3tog, k3; rep from * to last st, p1.
Row 3: K1, *p3, [k1, yo, k1] into next st; rep from * to last st, k1.
Row 4: P1, *k3, p3tog; rep from * to last st, p1.
Rep last 4 rows until square measures 6 in (15cm). Bind off.
Using D, make two more squares in same way.

Cobnut stitch squares (make 2)

Using size 3 (3.25mm) needles and B, cast on 32 sts.
Row 1 (RS): *P3, [k1, yo, k1] into next st; rep from * to end.
Rows 2 and 3: *P3, k3; rep from * to end.

Row 4: *P3tog, k3; rep from * to end.
Row 5: P.
Row 6: K.
Row 7: *P1, [k1, yo, k1] into next st, p2; rep from * to end.
Row 8: K2, *p3, k3; rep from * to last 4 sts, p3, k1.
Row 9: P1, *k3, p3; rep from * to last 5 sts, k3, p2.
Row 10: K2, *p3tog, k3; rep from * to last 4 sts, p3tog, k1.
Row 11: P.
Row 12: K.
Rep last 12 rows until square measures 6 in (15cm). Bind off.
Using E, make one more square in same way.

To finish

Weave in any loose yarn ends on knitted squares.
Lay squares out flat and gently steam.

Backing piece

For backing piece for bolster cover, cut a piece of fusible interfacing, 28 in (71cm) by 18 in (45cm).

Fabric patches

Cut a template for square fabric patches, 6 in (15cm) by 6 in (15cm) plus ½ in (1.5cm) all around for seam allowance.
Using template, cut the two complete squares, six half squares, and four quarter squares shown on diagram opposite, allowing 2 in (5cm) extra along buttonhole and

button band edges at top and bottom.

Patchwork arrangement

Iron fabric patches onto backing, then machine zigzag stitch around edges, using microfilament thread. Zigzag stitch knitted squares in place over seam allowances of fabric patches.

Button decoration

Sew one large button to center of each of six knitted squares, then sew four small buttons around each of these as shown.
Using seven large buttons, sew one to each corner of two square fabric patches at center of patchwork.

Bolster assembly

Turn under 2 in (5cm) at top and bottom of patchwork and stitch. Make two buttonholes evenly spaced on center patch of one end. Overlap buttonhole end over button band end and topstitch for approximately 4 in (10cm) at each end to secure. Sew on two large buttons to correspond with buttonholes.
Cut out two circles of fabric, each the size of bolster end plus ½ in (1.5cm) seam allowance all around. Turn patchwork cover wrong-side out and pin and stitch fabric ends in place. Turn right-side out and sew knitted bolster ends in place. Sew a tassel to center of each end of bolster, stitching it in place through a large button.

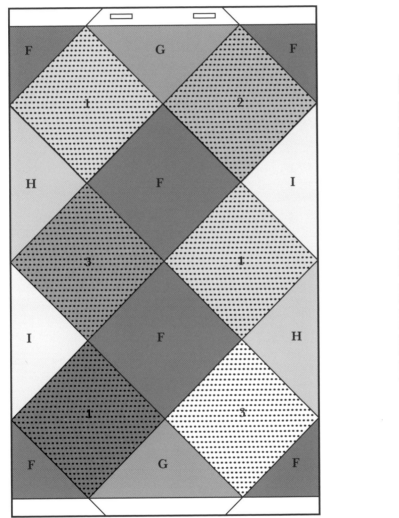

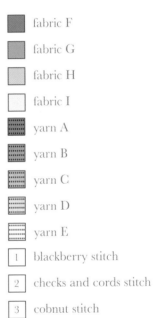

fabric F

fabric G

fabric H

fabric I

yarn A

yarn B

yarn C

yarn D

yarn E

1	blackberry stitch
2	checks and cords stitch
3	cobnut stitch

pooch cushion

Every pampered pet needs a gorgeous cushion to sit on and look adorable. Knitted in basic stockinette stitch, the animal-print motif can either be knitted in or embroidered on to the cushion. The main yarn is a luxurious cotton, but wool blends would work just as well. Along with a simple twisted braid and four tassels, a glittery knitted corsage ensures your pet is "Best in Show."

See pages 16–17

materials

Any medium-weight cotton or wool-blend yarn, such as
  Rowan *RYC Luxury Cotton DK*
  A: Six 1¾ oz (50g) balls in dark brown
  B: Three 1¾ oz (50g) balls in off-white
Any super-fine-weight metallic yarn, such as Rowan *Lurex Shimmer*
  C: One ⅞ oz (25g) ball in black
  D: Two ⅞ oz (25g) balls in white gold
  E: One ⅞ oz (25g) ball in bronze
Pair each of sizes 3 and 6 (3.25mm and 4mm) knitting needles
Pair each of sizes 3 and 5 (3.25mm and 3.75mm) double-pointed
  knitting needles
Large blunt-ended yarn needle
4 wooden beads, ¾ in (2cm) in diameter, for tassels
12 in (30cm) of black satin ribbon, 1 in (2.5cm) wide, for rosette
Large sew-on jewel or button
Sewing needle and sewing thread for stitching rosette
3 large snaps
Pillow form to fit finished cover

size

One size, approximately 16 in x 24 in (40cm x 60cm)

gauge

22 sts and 30 rows = 4 in (10cm) over St st using B and size 6 (4mm)
  needles or size necessary to obtain gauge.

pattern notes

- If you prefer to embroider the color pattern onto the knitting, follow the instructions for the embroidered top.
- When working the stockinette stitch color pattern from the chart, read odd-numbered rows (knit rows) from right to left and even-numbered rows (purl rows) from left to right.
- Work the color pattern using the intarsia technique, using a separate ball (or long length) of yarn for each area of color and twisting yarns on wrong side of work where colors change to avoid holes forming.

To make cushion base pieces (make 2)
Using size 6 (4mm) needles and A, cast on 132 sts.
Rib row 1: *K1, p1, rep from * to end.
Rep last row until work measures 1½ in (3.5cm) from cast-on edge, ending with RS facing for next row.
Beg with a k row, work 10 in (25cm) in St st.
Bind off.

To make cushion top
Using size 6 (4mm) needles and B, cast on 132 sts.
Embroidered top only:
Beg with a k row, work 16 in (40cm) in St st.
Top with knit-in pattern only:

Beg with a k row, work 2 rows in St st, ending with RS facing for next row.
Beg with a k row and chart row 1, work 75 rows following chart, ending with WS facing for next row.
Beg with a p row and using B only, cont in St st until work measures 16 in (40cm) from cast-on edge.
Both versions:
Bind off.

To make edging cords (make 2)
Using a pair of size 3 (3.25mm) double-pointed needles and one strand of D, cast on 6 sts.
Row 1 (RS): K.
Row 2 (RS): Without turning right needle, slide sts to right end of right needle and transfer this needle to

left hand, take yarn across WS of work from left to right and pull tightly, then k to end.
Rep last row until work measures approximately 2 yd (2m).
Slip sts onto a st holder and do not break off yarn.
Using a pair of size 5 (3.75mm) double-pointed needles and A, cast on 5 sts and make second cord in same way as first cord.

To make rosette circles (make 2)
Using size 6 (4mm) needles and A, cast on 28 sts.
Beg with a k row, work 2 rows in St st, ending with RS facing for next row.
Shape as foll:

Row 1 (RS): *K1, k into front and back of next st; rep from * to end.
Row 2 and every foll WS row: P.
Row 3: *K2, k into front and back of next st; rep from * to end.
Row 5: *K3, k into front and back of next st; rep from * to end.
Row 7: *K4, k into front and back of next st; rep from * to end.
Row 9: *K5, k into front and back of next st; rep from * to end.
Row 11: *K6, k into front and back of next st; rep from * to end.
Row 12: Rep row 2.
Bind off.
Using size 3 (3.25mm) needles and one strand of D, make second rosette circle in same way.

To make tassels (make 4)
Cut a generous number of lengths of A, D, and E, each approximately 12 in (30cm) long.
With lengths aligned, tie a strand of D around center.
Place a wooden bead in center of strands and fold them around bead. Then wrap a length of D around "neck" of tassel below bead. Keep winding to make a little band, then tie tightly.
Trim tassel.
Make three more tassels in same way.

To finish
Weave in any loose yarn ends.
Lay top and base pieces out flat and gently steam.
Embroidery
If embroidering color pattern, follow chart using duplicate st and gently steam again.
Cushion seams
Overlap two base pieces at ribbed edge to form a rectangle 16 in (40cm) by 24 in (60cm).
Then sew base to cushion top, using mattress stitch.
Edging cord
Twist two cords around each other and pin around edge of cushion.

Adjust cord lengths if necessary and bind off.
Sew twisted cord in place.
Rosettes
Sew row-end edges together on each rosette circle. Then work running stitch around cast-on edge of each circle, pull to gather, and secure end.
Place circle in D on top of circle in A and join together by stitching a large button or jewel through center.
Fold ribbon into a V-shape and sew to bottom of rosette as shown. Sew finished rosette to cushion top as shown.
Tassels
Sew a tassel to each corner of cushion.
Sew three snaps evenly spaced to overlapped rib edges of cushion base.
Insert pillow form.
Call for pup or puss!

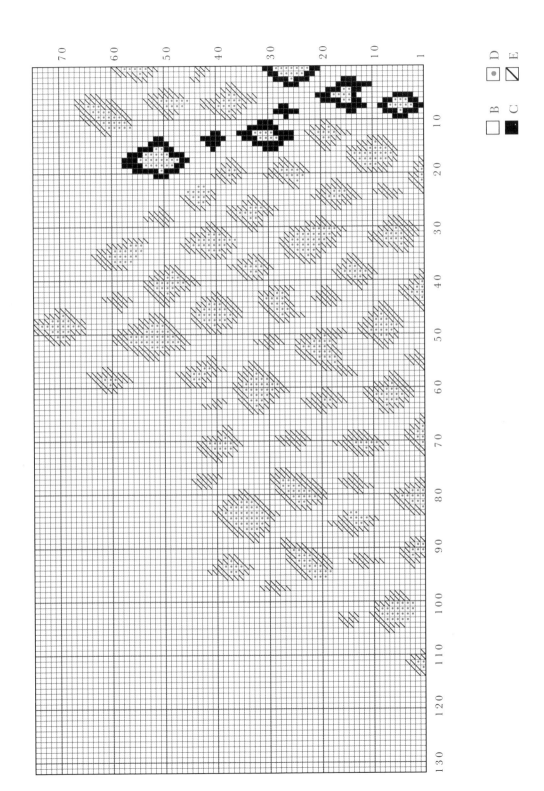

ornate slippers

These pretty slippers are made in vibrant mercerized cotton. Knitted in basic stockinette stitch, the simple, fully-fashioned shaping ensures a great fit and subtle detailing. Each slipper is embellished with fashionable grosgrain ribbon and a selection of sewn-on jewels for a stylish result.

See pages 18–19

materials

Any super-fine-weight mercerized cotton yarn, such as
    Yeoman *Cotton Cannele 4 Ply*
    One 8¾ oz (250g) cone in aubergine
Pair of size 6 (4mm) knitting needles
Large blunt-ended yarn needle
13 in (33cm) of grosgrain ribbon, 1½ in (4cm) wide
1 yd (1m) of satin ribbon, ½ in (1.5cm) wide
8 large square faceted sew-on jewels
2 small square faceted sew-on jewels
2 small round faceted sew-on jewels
Sewing needle and sewing thread for sewing on jewels

sizes

Size	small	medium	large	
Finished length	8	8¾	9½	in
	18.5	19.5	20.5	cm

Note: Slippers stretch to fit so that they fit snugly.

gauge

22 sts and 28 rows = 4 in (10cm) over St st using yarn doubled and
    size 6 (4mm) needles or size necessary to obtain gauge.

pattern note

The yarn is doubled throughout.

To make right sole

Using size 6 (4mm) needles and yarn doubled, cast on 5 sts.

Shape heel end

Work sole in St st as foll:

Row (RS): K.

Row 2: P1, M1, p to last st, M1, p1.

Row 3: K1, M1, k to last st, M1, k1.

Rep last 2 rows once more—*13 sts.*

Work even until sole measures 7¼ (7¾: 8) in/18.5 (19.5: 20.5)cm, ending with RS facing for next row.

Shape toe end

Next row (inc row) (RS): K2, M1, k to end.

Next row: P.

Rep last 2 rows 1 (3: 5) times more. —*15 (17: 19) sts.*

Work even until sole measures 7¼ (7¾: 8) in/18.5 (19.5: 20.5)cm from cast-on edge, ending with RS facing for next row.

Next row (RS): K2, k2tog, k to last 4 sts, k2tog tbl, k2.

Next row: P.

Rep last 2 rows until 7 sts remain. Bind off.

To make left sole

Work as for right sole, but work toe-end inc rows as foll:

Inc row (RS): K to last 2 sts, M1, k2.

To make uppers (make 2)

Using size 6 (4mm) needles and yarn doubled, cast on 6 sts.

Work upper in St st as foll:

Row 1 (WS): P.

Row 2: K2, M1, k to last 2 sts, M1, k2.

Row 3: P2, M1, p to last 2 sts, M1, p2.

Rep last 2 rows until there are 22 (26: 30) sts.

Next row: K2, M1, k to last 2 sts, M1, k2.

Next row: P.

Rep last 2 rows until there are 30 (32: 40) sts.

Work even until upper measures 3¼ (3½: 3¾) in/8 (9: 9.5)cm, ending with RS facing for next row.

Shape sides

Next row (RS): K14 (15: 19) and slip these sts onto a st holder, bind off next 2 sts, k to end.

Working on these 14 (15: 19) sts only, cont as foll:

Next row: P.

Next row: K3, k2tog, k to end.

Next row: P.

Rep last 2 rows until 11 (12: 16) sts remain.

Work even until upper measures 7 (8¼: 9) in/18 (21: 23)cm from cast-on edge, ending with RS facing for next row.

Next row (RS): K2, M1, k to end.

Work even for 3 rows.

Rep last 4 rows, twice more. —*14 (15: 19) sts.*

Work even until upper measures 8½ (9: 9¾) in/21.5 (23: 24.5)cm from cast-on edge. Bind off.

With WS facing, rejoin yarn to sts on holder and p to end.

Next row (RS): K to last 5 sts, sl 1, k1, psso, k3.

Next row: P.

Rep last 2 rows until 11 (12: 16) sts remain.

Work even until upper measures 7 (8¼: 9) in/18 (21: 23)cm from cast-on edge, ending with RS facing for next row.

Next row (RS): K to last 2 sts, M1, k2.

Work even for 3 rows.

Rep last 4 rows, twice more. —*14 (15: 19) sts.*

Work even until upper measures 8½ (9: 9¾) in/21.5 (23: 24.5)cm. Bind off.

To finish

Weave in any loose yarn ends.

Lay work out flat and gently steam.

Sew together bound-off edges of uppers with an outside seam to form heel.

With wrong sides together, pin sole to upper, easing to fit, and sew using mattress stitch.

Decoration

Cut grosgrain ribbon in half, fold ends in to center to make a double thickness, and press. Sew jewels to grosgrain ribbons as shown and sew to uppers.

Cut two 4 in (10cm) lengths of satin ribbon. Fold under ends of each piece, then fold in half widthwise to form a loop. Stitch one loop to heel seam on each slipper.

Use remaining satin ribbon to tie slippers together when not in use.

pleated ruffle cushion

This cushion is predominantly made up of a pretty knitted ruched panel worked in a gorgeous silk yarn. A chinoiserie satin panel is stitched to one end to create a modern style patchwork cushion that is trimmed with a velvet ribbon and then embellished with a corsage of silk fabric and knitted petals. The back consists of a classic cotton floral print and a plain silk fabric and is fastened with mother-of-pearl buttons.

See pages 20–21

materials

Any double-knitting-weight silk yarn, such as Debbie Bliss *Pure Silk*
   Two 1¾ oz (50g) hanks
Pair of size 6 (4mm) knitting needles
Medium-size blunt-ended yarn needle
Approximately ½ yd (50cm) in each of three different fabrics, such as:
   A: Chinoiserie satin jacquard
   B: Plain silk dupioni
   C: Cotton floral print
Approximately ½ yd (50cm) of velvet ribbon, ¾ in (2cm) wide
Matching thread for stitching cover
Three mother-of-pearl buttons
Pillow form, 12 in x 16 in (30cm x 40cm) to fit finished cover
Safety pin

size

One size, approximately 12 in x 16 in (30cm x 40cm)

gauge

24 sts and 32 rows = 4 in (10cm) over St st using size 6 (4mm) needles
   or size necessary to obtain gauge.

To make pleated cushion front
Using size 6 (4mm) needles, cast on
70 sts.
Beg with a k row, work 9 rows in
St st, ending with WS facing for
next row.
Beg pleat patt as foll:
Row 1 (WS): P5, *[with right
needle, pick up loop of next st
7 rows below and place on left
needle, then p tog picked-up loop
and next st on left needle] 4 times,
p4; rep from * to last st, p1.
Rows 2–8: Work 7 rows St st, beg
with a k row.
Row 9 (WS): P1, [pick up loop and
p as before] 4 times, *p4, [pick up
loop and p] 4 times, rep from * to
last st, p1.
Rows 10–16: Work 7 rows St st,
beg with a k row.
Rep last 16 rows until work
measures 8 in (20cm) from cast-on
edge, ending with RS facing for
next row.
Beg with a k row, work in St st until
work measures 12 in (30cm) from
cast-on edge.
Bind off.

Outer section of corsage
Using size 6 (4mm) needles, cast on
14 sts.

Row 1: K into front and back of
each stitch—*28 sts.*
Row 2: *K2, M1; rep from * to last
2 sts, k2—*41 sts.*
Row 3: *Cast on 15 sts onto left
needle, bind off 17 sts, slip st on
right needle back onto left needle;
rep from * to end.

Inner section of corsage
Work as for outer section until end
of row 2.
Row 3: *Cast on 9 sts onto left
needle, bind off 11 sts, slip st on
right needle back onto left needle;
rep from * to end.

To finish
Weave in any loose ends of yarn.
Cushion front
Cut a piece of fabric A 13 in
(33cm) by 5 in (13cm) and sew to
bound-off edge of knitted section,
stitching close to edge on knitting
and taking a $\frac{1}{2}$ in (1.5cm) seam on
fabric.
Using a zipper foot, sew velvet
ribbon over seam to cover it.
Cushion back
Cut a piece of fabric B 13 in
(33cm) by $12\frac{3}{4}$ in (32cm). To form
a buttonhole band, turn under $\frac{1}{2}$ in
(1.5cm) and then $2\frac{1}{2}$ in (6cm) along

one long edge and stitch.
Make three horizontal buttonholes
evenly spaced along band.
Cut a piece of fabric C 13 in
(33cm) by $12\frac{1}{4}$ in (31cm). To form
button band, turn under $\frac{1}{2}$ in
(1.5cm) and then 2in (5cm) along
on one long edge and stitch.
Place buttonhole band section over
button band section so back pieces
are overlapping to create a cushion
back 17 in (43cm) wide. Baste layers
to together to hold them in place.
With right sides of back and front
together, pin and baste, then sew all
around edge. Turn right-side out.
Sew on buttons.
Insert pillow form.
Corsage
Cut two pieces of fabric C
approximately same size as knitted
corsage sections and cut them to
make a fringe.
Place fabric fringe pieces on top of
knitted fringe, pleat into a circle,
and sew to secure.
Pin finished corsage to front of
cushion with a safety pin.

scented squares

These scented sachets are made in beautiful fine silk, in two different stitch patterns, and worked with glass beads, and are slipped over an envelope organza bag filled with a potpourri of lavender or rose petals to create something exquisitely pretty and enduring. Each knitted pillow features a turned hem that is tied with satin ribbons to finish.

See pages 22–23

materials

Any super-fine-weight silk yarn, such as Jaeger *Silk 4 Ply*
    One 1¾ oz (50g) ball
Approximately 1,300 beads, for scented square with all-over beads
Approximately 220 beads, for scented square with knots and beads
Pair of size 3 (3mm) knitting needles
Medium-size blunt-ended yarn needle
Small piece of organza and matching sewing thread to make
    inner bag
Lavender or rose petals to fill inner bag
Satin ribbons

size

One size, approximately 5 in x 5 in (12.5cm x 12.5cm)

gauge

Scented square with all-over beads: 28 sts and 52 rows = 4 in (10cm)
    over beaded St st using size 3 (3mm) needles or size necessary
    to obtain gauge.
Scented square with knots and beads: 28 sts and 40 rows = 4 in (10cm)
    over beaded knot pattern using size 3 (3mm) needles or size
    necessary to obtain gauge.

pattern note

Before starting to knit, thread the beads onto the yarn. To do this,
thread a sewing needle that will pass through the bead with
sewing thread, knot the ends of the thread, and put the yarn
through this loop. Thread the beads onto the needle and slide
them along onto the yarn until they are all threaded on.

special abbreviations

bead 1 = bring yarn to front (RS) of work between two needles, slip bead up next to st just worked and slip next st purlwise from left needle to right needle to leave bead in front of slipped st, then take yarn to back (WS) of work between two needles.

make knot = p3tog leaving sts on left needle, then k same 3 sts tog, p them tog again and slip sts off left needle.

To make scented square with all-over beads

Using size 3 (3mm) needles, cast on 42 sts.

Beg with a k row, work 6 rows in St st, ending with RS facing for next row.

Next row (ridge row) (RS): P, to form foldline ridge.

Next row: P.

Now add beads where indicated as foll:

Row 1 (RS): K2, *bead 1, k1; rep from * to last 2 sts, k2.

Row 2: P.

Row 3: K3, *bead 1, k1; rep from * to last st, k1.

Row 4: P.

Rep last 4 rows until work measures 10 in (25cm) from ridge row, ending with WS facing for next row.

Next row (ridge row) (WS): K, to form foldline ridge on RS.

Beg with a k row, work 6 rows in St st.

Bind off.

To make scented square with knots and beads

Using size 3 (3mm) needles, cast on 42 sts.

Beg with a k row, work 6 rows in St st, ending with RS facing for next row.

Next row (ridge row) (RS): P, to form foldline ridge.

Next row: P.

Now make knots and add beads where indicated as foll:

Row 1 (RS): K1, *make knot, k3; rep from * to last 5 sts, make knot, k2.

Row 2: P.

Row 3: K2, *bead 1, k5; rep from * to last 4 sts, bead 1, k3.

Row 4: P.

Row 5: K4, *make knot, k3; rep from * to last 2 sts, k2.

Row 6: P.

Row 7: *K5, bead 1; rep from * to last 6 sts, k6.

Row 8: P.

Rep last 8 rows until work measures 10 in (25cm) from ridge row, ending with WS facing for next row.

Next row (ridge row) (WS): K, to form foldline ridge on RS.

Beg with a k row, work 6 rows in St st.

Bind off.

To finish both pillows

Weave in any loose yarn ends. Lay work out flat and gently steam on WS to avoid damaging beads. Fold in half widthwise and sew both side seams.

Turn top edge to inside along ridge row and sew in place.

Sew a length of ribbon to each side of opening.

Inner bag

Cut a strip of organza 6 in (15.5cm) by 11 in (29cm). Fold in half widthways and sew sides taking ½ in (1.5cm) seams. Turn right-side out and fill with lavender or rose petals. Slip stitch opening closed. Insert bag into knitted pillow cover.

chinoiserie throw

This lavish throw consists of seven fabric panels, four of which are pieced and have three sections of appliqué knitted lace in each panel. The back of the throw is made up of larger fabric pieces, all with a vintage aesthetic.

See pages 24–25

materials

Any super-fine-weight cotton yarn, such as Yeoman *Cotton Cannele 4 Ply*
> **A:** Small amount of four different colors—tangerine, dusty pink, light pink, and light sage

Any double-knitting-weight silk yarn, such as Debbie Bliss *Pure Silk*
> **B:** One 1¾ oz (50g) hank in mauve

Pair of size 6 (4mm) knitting needles

Five assorted fabrics (and matching thread) for patchwork, such as
> **A:** Chinoiserie silk in three colorways
> **B:** Floral print cotton lawn
> **C:** Silk dupioni

Ten 1-yd (1m) lengths of assorted velvet, satin ribbons and sequins

Fusible interfacing

Microfilament sewing thread

size

One size, approximately 50¼ in x 50¼ in (127cm x 127cm)

gauge

29 sts and 36 rows = 4 in (10cm) over St st using size 3 (3.25mm) needles or size necessary to obtain gauge and yarn A.

24 sts and 30 rows = 4 in (10cm) over St st using size 6 (4mm) needles or size necessary to obtain gauge and yarn B.

pattern notes

- Make 12 assorted knitted squares using the stitch patterns on the opposite page, in a variety of yarns and colors and introducing colored stripes as desired.

- Make each square either 9½ in (24cm) long or 9½ in (24cm) wide so they can be appliquéd in place either vertically or horizontally across a 9½ in (24cm) panel. For vertical squares, work a swatch to determine how many stitches to cast on for a 9½ in (24cm) width.

To make knit patches
Using size 6 (4mm) needles, make 12 knitted patches (see pattern notes).

Cell stitch
Cast on a multiple of 4 sts plus 3 sts.
Row 1 (RS): K2, *yo, sl 1, k2tog, psso, yo, k1; rep from * to last st, k1.
Row 2: P.
Row 3: K1, k2 tog, yo, k1, *yo, sl 1, k2tog, psso, yo, k1; rep from * to last 3 sts, yo, sl 1, k1, psso, k1.
Rows 4 and 5: K.
Row 6: P.
Row 7: K.
Row 8: P.
Rep last 8 rows to form patt.

Van Dyke stitch
Cast on a multiple of 10 sts plus 1 st.
Row 1 (RS): K1, *yo, k3, sl 1, k2tog, psso, k3, yo, k1; rep from *.
Row 2 every WS row: Purl.
Row 3: K1, *k1, yo, k2, sl 1, k2tog, psso, k2, yo, k2; rep from *.
Row 5: K1, *k2, yo, k1, sl 1, k2tog, psso, k1, yo, k3; rep from *.
Row 7: K1, *k3, yo, sl 1, k2tog, psso, yo, k4; rep from *.
Row 8: Rep row 2.
Rep last 8 rows to form patt.

Little shell pattern
Cast on a multiple of 6 sts plus 2 sts.
Row 1 (RS): K.
Row 2: P.
Row 3: K2, *yo, p1, p3tog, yo, k2, rep from *.
Row 4: P.
Rep last 4 rows to form patt.

Undulating lacy rib
Cast on a multiple of 9 sts plus 2 sts
Rows 1, 3, 5, 7, and 9: *K2, yo, k1, yo, k2, k2tog tbl, k2tog; rep from * to last 2 sts, k2.
Row 2 and every foll WS row: P.
Rows 11, 13, 15, 17, and 19: *K2, k2tog tbl, k2tog, k2, yo, k1, yo; rep from * to last 2 sts, k2.
Row 20: Rep row 2.
Rep last 20 rows to form patt.

Openwork rib
Cast on a multiple of 4 sts plus 1 st.
Row 1: K1, *k3, p1; rep from *.
Row 2: *K1, p3; rep from * to last st, p1.
Row 3: K1, *yo, sl 1, k2tog, psso, yo, p1; rep from *.
Row 4: Rep row 2.
Rep last 4 rows to form patt.

To finish
Gently press 12 knitted squares. Thread ribbons and sequins through lace eyelets to embellish knits.

Patchwork top
Cut patches 10½ in (27cm) wide from A, B, and C. Iron fusible interfacing onto WS of each piece. Taking ½ in (1.5cm) seams on fabric throughout, sew together patches into four panels, each 10½ in (27cm) wide by 48¾ in (123cm) long.
Cut three strips of fabric A, each 4¼ in (11cm) by 48¾ in (123cm). Then stitch three narrow strips to four pieced panels, alternating the widths.
Using microfilament thread, machine zigzag three knitted pieces in random positions to each of four wide panels, stretching knitting to fit if necessary and leaving ½ in (1.5cm) uncovered around outer edge of top for edging seam.

Patchwork backing
From A, cut four pieces each 19¾ in (50cm) square; then from C, cut two pieces each 11¼ in (29cm) by 19¾ in (50cm), and one strip 11¼ in (29cm) by 48¾ in (123cm). Iron fusible interfacing to each backing piece. Make two panels, each with two A squares sewn to either side of one rectangle in C.
Sew pieced panels to either side of strip in C to make a 48¾ in 123cm) square.
With wrong sides together, place patchwork top on top of backing, pin and stitch around edges.

Patchwork edging
From assorted fabrics, cut 24 rectangles, each 3½ in (10cm) by 9½ in (25cm). Piece these rectangles together lengthwise to make four long strips of six rectangles each. Trim two strips to 48¾ in (123cm) and two to 51¼ in (130cm).
Press ½ in (1.5cm) onto wrong side along one long edge of each strip. With right sides together, and taking ½ in (1.5cm) seams, stitch unpressed edge of two shorter edging strips to top and bottom of throw. Fold these strips over onto back of throw and slip stitch pressed edge to backing along stitching line.
Repeat this on other two edges, folding under raw edges at corners.

boudoir cushion

Pretty *and* pink! This is the perfect piece to adorn a favorite bedroom chair. It is knitted in smooth, silky cotton yarn, and a simple stitch decorates the top and complements the frilled edging. Glass beads further embellish the skirt and satin bows tie the cushion stylishly and practically in place.

See pages 26–27

materials

Any lightweight cotton-blend yarn, such as Debbie Bliss *Cathay*
  Eight 1¾ oz (50g) balls
Pair of size 5 (3.75mm) knitting needles
Size 5 (3.75mm) circular knitting needle for edging
Large blunt-ended yarn needle
Pillow form 14 in x 14 in (35.5cm x 35.5cm) to fit finished cover
Approximately 500 small (3mm) pink glass seed beads
Approximately 2¾ yd (2.5m) of pink satin ribbon, 2 in (5cm) wide

size

One size, 14 in x 14 in (35.5cm x 35.5cm)

gauge

22 sts and 30 rows = 4 in (10cm) over St st using size 5 (3.75mm)
  needles or size necessary to obtain gauge.

special abbreviations

make knot = p3tog leaving sts on left needle, then k same 3 sts tog,
  p them tog again and slip sts off left needle.

Knot pattern
Row 1 (RS): K.
Row 2 and every foll WS row: P.
Row 3: K1, * make knot, k3; rep from * to last 4 sts, make knot, k1.
Row 5: K.
Row 7: K4, * make knot, k3; rep from * to last st, k1.
Row 8: P.
Rep last 8 rows to form knot patt.

To make cushion top
Using size 5 (3.75mm) needles, cast on 77 sts.
Beg with a k row, work 15 rows in St st, ending with WS facing for next row.
Next row (WS): P11, k55, p11.
Next row (RS): K11, p1, work row 1 of knot patt over next 53 sts, p1, k11.
Next row: P11, k1, work row 2 of knot patt over next 53 sts, k1, p11.
Cont with sts and knot patt as set until work measures 12 in (30cm) from cast-on edge, ending with RS facing for next row.
Next row (RS): K11, p55, k11.
Beg with a p row, work 15 rows in St st.
Bind off.

To make cushion base
Using size 5 (3.75mm) needles, cast on 77 sts.

Beg with a k row, work in St st for 14 in (35cm).
Bind off.

To make cushion edging
With RS of work facing and using size 5 (3.75mm) needles, pick up and k 79 sts along bound-off edge of cushion top (back edge of cushion top).
Row 1 (WS): K4, *p1, k4; rep from * to end.
Row 2: P4, *M1, k1, M1, p4; rep from * to end.
Rows 3, 5, and 7: K4, *p3, k4; rep from * to end.
Rows 4 and 6: P4, *k3, p4; rep from * to end.
Row 8: P4, *[k1, M1] twice, k1, p4; rep from * to end.
Row 9: K4, *p5, k4; rep from * to end.
Row 10: P4, *k5, p4; rep from * to end.
Rows 11–18: Rep rows 9 and 10 four times.
Row 19: Rep row 9.
Row 20: P4, *k1, M1, k3, M1, k1, p4; rep from * to end.
Row 21: K4, *p7, k4; rep from * to end.
Row 22: P4, *k7, p4; rep from * to end.
Rows 23–30: Rep rows 21 and 22 four times.

Row 31: Rep row 21.
Work simple picot bind-off as foll:
Next row: Bind off 4 sts, * slip st on right needle back onto left needle, k twice into this st, bind off 4 sts; rep from * to end.
Work edging around remaining three sides of cushion as foll:
With RS of cushion top facing and using size 5 (3.75) circular needle, pick up and k 78 sts along one side edge of cushion, 78 sts along cast-on edge, and 78 sts along remaining side edge of cushion —*234 sts.*
Work 31-row edging patt and picot bind-off on these sts.

To finish
Weave in any loose yarn ends.
Lay work out flat and gently steam.
Sew cushion base to top along three sides, using mattress stitch.
Insert pillow form and sew final seam.
Cut ribbon into four pieces. Fold under one end of each piece to neaten and stitch a pair at each side of opening at back of cushion, under edging. Tie in a large bow.
Stitch a small glass bead to each point of picot edge.

tea party tea cozy

materials

$3\frac{1}{4}$ yd (3m) of $27\frac{1}{2}$-in (70cm) wide tulle fabric, cut into a continuous strip
Pair of size 13 (9mm) knitting needles
$\frac{1}{2}$ yd (50cm) of $27\frac{1}{2}$-in (70cm) wide chinoiserie fabric for lining
Elastic thread
$\frac{1}{2}$ yd (50cm) of organza ribbon, $1\frac{1}{2}$ in (4cm) wide

size

One size, approximately 17 in (43cm) in circumference and 9 in (23cm) tall

gauge

12 sts and 20 rows = 4 in (10cm) over garter st using size 13 (9mm) needles
or size necessary to obtain gauge.

pattern note

To cut the tulle into a continuous strip of "yarn," start by laying it out flat.
Working from right to left, cut the tulle 1 in (2.5cm) from the bottom edge
to within $\frac{3}{4}$ in (2cm) of the left edge. Then cut from left to right 1 in
(2.5cm) away from the first cut, again leaving $\frac{3}{4}$ in (2cm) uncut at the right
edge. Continue in this way, rolling the strip into a ball as you work.

**To make tea cozy pieces
(make 2)**
Using size 13 (9mm) needles, cast
on 26 sts.
Work in garter st (k every row) for
9 in (23cm).
Bind off.

To finish
Using knitted pieces as templates,
cut two pieces of lining fabric,
allowing $\frac{1}{2}$ in (1.5cm) extra all
around. Turn under edges on
lining pieces and sew them to
knitted pieces.
With wrong sides together, sew

seams, leaving gaps for spout and
handle. Run a double line of elastic
thread through tulle knitting only,
2 in (5cm) down from top, and
gently gather up.
Make a floppy bow with organza
ribbon and sew to tea-cozy on
gathered neck.

See pages 28–29

jacquard cushion

Inspired by boudoir wallpaper patterns, this petite cushion is knitted in two colors using a simple stranding technique.
It is worked in mercerized cotton, backed in sumptuous velvet, and trimmed with either braid or tassels.

See pages 30–31

materials

Any super-fine-weight mercerized cotton yarn, such as
>   Yeoman *Cotton Cannele 4 Ply*
>   **A:** One 8¾ oz (250g) cone in black
>   **B:** One 8¾ oz (250g) cone in turquoise

Pair of size 3 (3.25mm) knitting needles
Medium-size blunt-ended yarn needle
Approximately ½ yd (50cm) of black velvet fabric and matching
  sewing thread for cushion back
Pillow form 12 in x 12 in (30.5cm x 30.5cm) to fit finished cover
1½ yd (1.3m) of braid trimming for edging (optional)

size

One size, approximately 12 in x 12 in (30.5cm x 30.5cm)

gauge

29 sts and 36 rows = 4 in (10cm) over pattern using size 3 (3.25mm)
  needles or size necessary to obtain gauge.

pattern notes

- For the reverse colorway, use A for B and B for A. The yarn amount
  specified is enough for both cushions.
- When working the stockinette stitch color pattern from the chart,
  read odd-numbered rows (knit rows) from right to left and even-
  numbered rows (purl rows) from left to right.
- Work the color pattern using the stranding (Fair Isle) technique,
  stranding the yarn not in use loosely across the back of the work. Do
  not carry the yarn over more than three stitches at a time, but weave
  it under and over the color being worked.

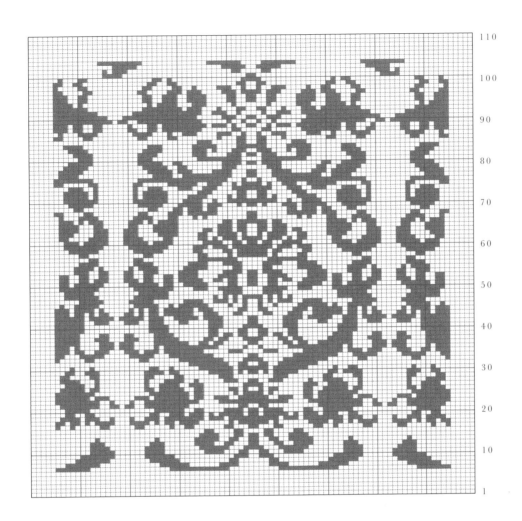

To make cushion front

Using size 3 (3.25mm) needles and
B, cast on 90 sts.
Beg with a k row and chart row 1,
work 110 rows following chart.
Bind off.

To finish

Weave in any loose yarn ends.
Lay work out flat and gently steam.
For cushion back, cut two pieces of
fabric, each $10\frac{1}{2}$ in (27cm) by 13 in
(33cm).
Along one long edge of each piece
fold $\frac{1}{2}$ in (1.5cm) to wrong side twice
and stitch to form a double hem.
Lay knitting right-side up and place
both back pieces wrong-side up on
top, so that raw edges extend $\frac{1}{2}$ in
(1.5cm) past edges of knitting and
hemmed edges overlap at center.
Pin and stitch around all sides,
taking a $\frac{1}{2}$ in (1.5cm) seam on
fabric and stitching close to edge on
knitting. Turn right-side out.

Tassels (optional)

Using a piece of cardboard 4 in
(10cm) square and A, make four
tassels as for tassel on page 97, but
tying tassels $\frac{3}{4}$ in (2cm) from top.
Sew one tassel to each corner of
cushion, or sew braid around edge.
Insert pillow form.

dress hanger

Make this special decorative hanger to display a vintage dress, as a gift for a bride or new homeowner, or simply to enjoy for your own use. Worked in two pieces, the knitted cover has a picot edge with knitted-in beads and sequins and random longer picots around the center hook. The hook is covered in ribbon, which is then tied around the neck in a bow.

See pages 32–33

materials

Any super-fine-weight mercerized cotton yarn, such as
   Yeoman *Cotton Cannele 4 Ply*
   One 8¾ oz (250g) cone
Approximately 5½ yd (5m) of ribbon, ¼ in (7mm) wide
Two pairs of size 3 (3.25mm) knitting needles
Medium-size blunt-ended yarn needle
Approximately 100 small (3mm) green or pink glass seed beads
Approximately 100 small (5mm) green or pink glass bugle beads
Approximately 100 small (5mm) shiny green or pink sequins
Standard-size padded and covered coat-hanger, approximately
   17 in (43cm) long x 5 in (13cm) around
Sewing needle and sewing thread to sew on extra beads and sequins

size

One size, to fit standard coat-hanger

gauge

29 sts and 32 rows = 4 in (10cm) over St st using size 3 (3.25mm)
   needles or size necessary to obtain gauge.

To make hanger cover

Using size 3 (3.25mm) needles, cast on 124 sts.

Back of cover

Beg with a k row, work 19 rows in St st, ending with WS facing for next row.

Cut yarn leaving a long end, leave these sts on needle, and set aside.

Front of cover

Thread approximately 60 beads and sequins onto yarn.

Using size 3 (3.25mm) needles and yarn threaded with beads and sequins, cast on 124 sts.

Pushing beads and sequins along yarn (to use for picot bind-off) and beg with a k row, work 20 rows in St st, ending with RS facing for next row.

Do not cut yarn.

Join back and front

Join back and front of cover as foll: Hold two needles with back and front on them in your left hand, the back behind the front with WS together and needle points facing to right, then with a third needle k to end of row, working 1 st from front needle tog with same st from needle behind—*124 sts*.

Picot bind-off

Remembering to transfer st on right needle to left needle after each bind-off, work picot bind-off as foll: [Cast on 3 sts (onto left needle), insert bead/sequin, bind off next 6 sts] 19 times.

Cast on 26 sts, placing bead/sequin on each of last 4 sts, bind off next 28 sts.

Cast on 33 sts, placing bead/sequin on each of last 4 sts, bind off next 35 sts.

Cast on 44 sts, placing bead/sequin on each of last 4 sts, bind off next 46 sts.

Cast on 40 sts, placing bead/sequin on each of last 4 sts, bind off next 42 sts.

Cast on 20 sts, placing bead/sequin on each of last 4 sts, bind off next 22 sts.

[Cast on 3 sts, insert bead/sequin, bind off next 6 sts] 19 times. Fasten off.

To finish

Weave in any loose yarn ends. Lay work out flat and gently steam. Sew seam on knitted cover, leaving one short end open.

Remove hook and push hanger into cover.

Sew short end closed.

Screw hook back into hanger, gently pushing through knitting.

Embellishments

Cover hook with satin ribbon by wrapping around hook in blanket-stitch fashion and secure with small sewing stitches.

Tie ribbon around neck of hook and tie in a bow. Sew a few sequins onto ribbon.

Embellish long tendrils randomly with beads and sequins to create pretty dangling shapes.

knot stitch cushion

materials

Any super-fine-weight mercerized cotton yarn, such as
>Yeoman *Cotton Cannele 4 Ply*
>One 8¾ oz (250g) cone

Pair of size 8 (5mm) knitting needles

Medium-size blunt-ended yarn needle

Pillow form 18 in x 18 in (45.5cm x 45.5cm) to fit finished cover

¾ yd (50cm) of silk fabric to cover pillow form

size

One size, approximately 18 in x 18 in (45.5cm x 45.5cm)

gauge

17 sts = 4 in (10cm) over knot stitch pattern using size 8 (5mm)
needles or size necessary to obtain gauge.

To make cushion front

Using size 8 (5mm) needles, cast on
77 sts.

Beg with a k row, work 2 rows in
St st, ending with RS facing for
next row.

Beg knot stitch patt as foll:

Row 1 (RS): K3, *yo, sl 1, k2tog,
psso, yo, k1; rep from * to last
2 sts, k2.

Row 2: P.

Row 3: K2, k2tog, yo, k1,
*yo, sl 1, k2tog, psso, yo, k1; rep
from * to last 4 sts, yo, sl 1, k1,
psso, k2.

Row 4: P.

Rep last 4 rows until work measures
17¾ in (44cm) from cast-on edge,
ending with RS facing for next row.

Beg with a k row, work 2 rows in
St st.

Bind off.

To make cushion back

Work cushion back exactly as for
cushion front.

To finish

Weave in any loose yarn ends.

Lay work out flat and gently steam.

Pillow form covering

Cut two pieces of fabric 19 in (48cm)
square.

With right sides together, stitch
around three sides, taking a ½ in
(1.5cm) seam. Turn right-side out.
Insert pillow form and slip stitch
opening closed.

Knitted cover

With wrong sides facing, sew three
seams of cushion cover, using
mattress stitch.

Insert pillow form and sew last
seam.

See pages 34–35

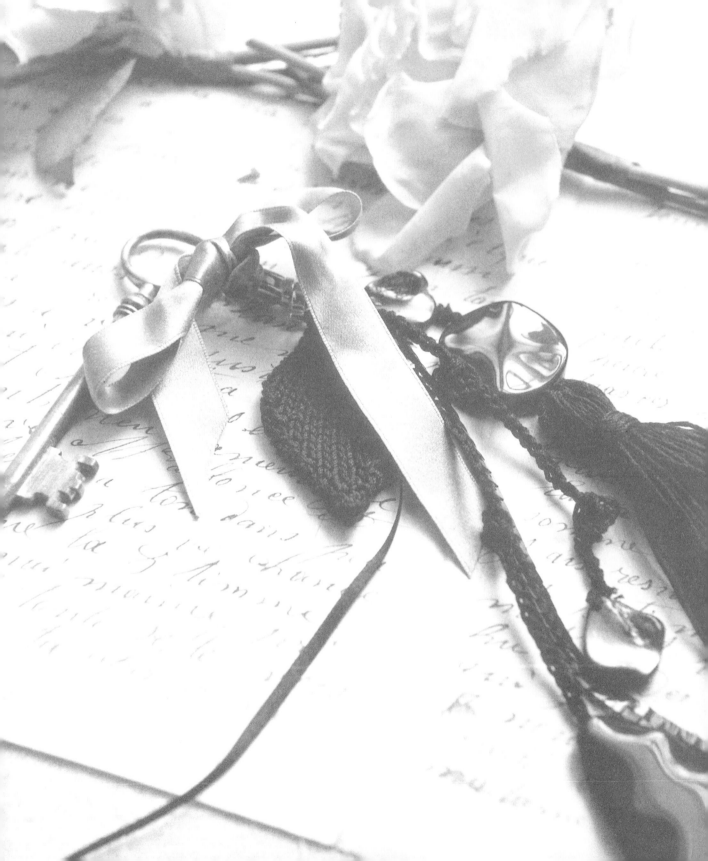

key fob

This small project makes a great gift for a new homeowner. It consists of strands of knitted leaf motifs and I-cords with bobbles and is decorated with beads and stones, sequins, ribbon, and a tassel to create an individual, stylish, and pretty piece.

See pages 36–37

materials

Any super-fine-weight mercerized cotton yarn, such as
Yeoman *Cotton Cannele 4 Ply*
Pair of size 2 (2.75mm) knitting needles
1 small-size (15mm) natural irregular black bead
1 medium-size (30mm) natural irregular black bead
1 large-size (50mm) natural irregular black bead
1 small-size (15mm) natural stone bead
8 in (20cm) of a strand of black sequins
8 in (20cm) of very narrow black satin ribbon
$^1/_2$ yd (50cm) of taupe satin ribbon, $^1/_2$ in (1cm) wide
Snap hook

To make leaf shapes (make 2)
Using size 2 (2.75mm) needles, cast
on 3 sts
Row 1 (RS): K.
Row 2 and every foll WS row: P.
Row 3: [K1, M1] twice, k1.
Row 5: K2, M1, k1, M1, k2.
Row 7: K3, M1, k1, M1, k3.
Row 9: K4, M1, k1, M1, k4.
Row 11: K5, M1, k1, M1, k5—*13 sts.*
Row 13: Sl 1, k1, psso, k to last
2 sts, k2tog.
Row 15: Rep row 13.
Row 17: Rep row 13.
Row 19: Rep row 13.

Row 21: Rep row 13—*3 sts.*
Row 23: Sl 1, k2tog, psso.
Fasten off.
Make second leaf shape in the
same way.

I-cord with bobbles (make 2)
Using size 2 (2.75mm) needles, cast
on 1 st, leaving a long yarn end (to
secure cord to snap hook).
Work this st in garter st (k every
row) until cord measures $^3/_4$ in (2cm).
Next row (bobble row) [K into
front and back of st] twice, k into
front of st again—*5 sts.*

K 1 row.
Next row P5tog—*1 st rem.*
Cont as set, working a bobble as
before at random intervals between
rows of garter st until cord
measures approximately 3 in
(7.5cm) from cast-on edge.
Fasten off, leaving a long yarn end
(to go through bead).
Make a second cord in same way
approximately $4^1/_4$ in (11cm) long.

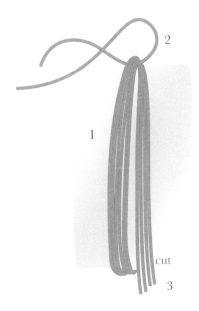

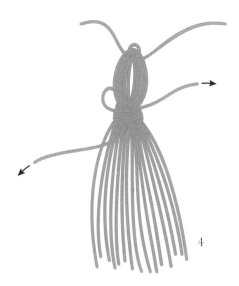

To make tassel

Cut a piece of cardboard 5 in (13cm) long (or length of tassel required) and wrap a generous amount of yarn around it.

Wrap a separate length of yarn a few times around strands at one end of cardboard and knot, leaving long enough loose ends for stitching tassel in place.

Cut strands at other end of tassel. Wrap another length of yarn around tassel, approximately ½ in (1.5cm) from top (to form a "neck"), linking and securing ends under wrapping.

To finish

Thread large bead onto longest length of I-cord and attach this cord to snap hook by folding over top and securing with a small stitch. Thread smaller natural stone onto shorter length of I-cord and attach this cord to snap hook in same way. Next, attach lengths of sequins and narrow satin ribbon to snap hook in same way as cords.

Thread end at top of tassel through medium bead, then through other natural stone. Attach tassel to snap hook with a knot and secure with a small stitch.

Sew two leaf shapes together around edges, fold top over snap hook, and secure with a few small stitches.

Finally, thread silk ribbon through the snap hook and tie in a bow.

pearl button and lace sequin cushions

These are the simplest of cushions, made in the most beautiful of yarns. For one, whisper-soft silk mohair in the palest pearl shade is embellished with natural mother-of-pearl buttons, randomly scattered for added glamour. To complement the first, the second cushion is worked in the same yarn, crafted into a delicate lace and scattered with silver sequins.

See pages 38–39

materials

pearl button cushion

Any fine-weight mohair-blend yarn, such as Rowan *Kidsilk Haze*
 Four ⅞ oz (25g) balls
Pair of size 5 (3.75mm) knitting needles
Approximately 70 mother-of-pearl buttons in assorted sizes

lace sequin cushion

Any fine-weight 4 ply mohair-blend yarn, such as Rowan *Kidsilk Haze*
 Two ⅞ oz (25g) balls
Pair of size 8 (5mm) knitting needles
Approximately 100 small (5mm) and medium (10mm) shiny silver sequins
7 small mother-of-pearl buttons
35½ in (50cm) of 19¾ in (90cm) wide silk fabric and matching sewing thread

both cushions

Medium-size blunt-ended yarn needle
Pillow form to fit finished cover

size

Pearl button cushion: One size, approximately 16 in x 16 in (40cm x 40cm)
Lace sequin cushion: One size, approximately 16 in x 12 in (40cm x 30cm)

gauge

Pearl button cushion: 22 sts and 30 rows = 4 in (10cm) over St st using yarn
 doubled and size 5 (3.75mm) needles or size necessary to obtain gauge.
Lace sequin cushion: 19 sts and 24 rows = 4 in (10cm) over stitch pattern
 using size 8 (5mm) needles or size necessary to obtain gauge.

stitches
lace stitch pattern
Row 1 (WS): K3, p to last 3 sts, k3.
Row 2: K5, *yo, k2, sl 1, k1, psso, k2tog, k2, yo, k1; rep from * to
last 4 sts, k4.
Row 3: K3, p to last 3 sts, k3.
Row 4: K4, *yo, k2, sl 1, k1, psso, k2tog, k2, yo, k1; rep from * to
last 5 sts, k5.
Rep last 4 rows to form lace stitch patt.

To make button cushion
Using size 5 (3.75mm) needles and
two strands of yarn held tog, cast
on 81 sts.
Row 1 (RS): *K2, p1; rep from *
to end.
Row 2: *K1, p2; rep from * to end.
Rep last 2 rib rows until work
measures 1 in (2.5cm), ending with
RS facing for next row.
Beg with a k row, work in St st until
work measures 34½ in (87.5cm)
from cast-on edge, ending with RS
facing for next row.
Work in rib as for cast-on edge for
1 in (2.5cm). Bind off in rib.

To make lace sequin cushion
Using size 8 (5mm) needles, cast on
153 sts.

Work ¾ in (2cm) in lace stitch patt,
ending with RS facing for next row.
Next row (buttonhole row): K1,
yo, k2tog, patt to end.
Cont in patt and work 6 more
buttonholes approximately 1½ in
(4cm) apart **and at the same
time** cont until work measures
12 in (30cm) from cast-on edge,
ending with WS facing for next row.
Bind off.

To finish both cushions
Weave in any loose yarn ends.
Lay work out flat and gently steam.
Button cushion
Fold edges into center, overlapping
by 2 in (5cm).
Sew side seams with mattress stitch,
working through all layers.

Scatter buttons randomly over
cushion front and sew in place.
Insert pillow form.
Lace cushion
Fold edges into center, overlapping
by width of garter stitch borders.
Sew side seams with mattress stitch,
working through all layers.
Scatter sequins randomly over
cushion front and sew in place.
Sew on buttons to match
buttonholes.
For fabric pillow form cover, cut
two pieces of silk fabric, each 17 in
(43cm) square. With right sides of
fabric together, stitch around three
sides, taking a ½ in (1.5cm) seam.
Turn right-side out.
Insert pillow form, slip stitch seam
closed, and insert in lace cover.

yarns

Although I have recommended specific yarns for the projects in the book, you can use substitutes if you like. A description of each of the yarns used is given below.

If you decide to use an alternative yarn, purchase a substitute yarn that is as close as possible to the original in thickness, weight, and texture so that it will work with the pattern instructions. Buy only one ball to start with, so you can test the effect. Calculate the number of balls you will need by yardage rather than by weight. The recommended knitting-needle size and knitting gauge on the yarn labels are extra guides to the yarn thickness.

To obtain Debbie Bliss, Rowan (and Jaeger) or Yeoman yarns, go to the websites below to find a store in your area:

www.knitrowan.com for Rowan
www.debbieblissonline.com for Debbie Bliss
www.yeoman-yarns.co.uk for Yeoman

Debbie Bliss *Cathay*
A lightweight cotton-blend yarn
Recommended needle size: size 5 (3.75mm)
Gauge: 22 sts and 30 rows = 4 in (10cm) over knitted St st
Ball size: 109 yd (100m) per 1¾ oz (50g) ball
Yarn specification: 50% cotton, 35% viscose microfiber, 15% silk

Debbie Bliss *Pure Silk*
A double-knitting-weight silk yarn
Recommended needle size: size 6 (4mm)
Gauge: 24 sts and 30 rows = 4 in (10cm) over knitted St st
Hank size: 137 yd (125m) per 1¾ oz (50g) ball
Yarn specification: 100% pure silk

Jaeger *Siena*
A super-fine-weight mercerized cotton yarn
Recommended needle size: size 2–3 (2.75–3.25mm)
Gauge: 28 sts and 38 rows = 4 in (10cm) over knitted St st
Ball size: 153 yd (140m) per 1¾ oz (50g) ball
Yarn specification: 100% mercerized cotton

Jaeger *Silk 4 Ply*
A super-fine-weight silk yarn
Recommended needle size: size 3 (3mm)
Gauge: 28 sts and 38 rows = 4 in (10cm) over knitted St st
Ball size: 203 yd (186m) per 1¾ oz (50g) ball
Yarn specification: 100% silk

Rowan *Cotton Glacé*
A fine-weight cotton yarn
Recommended needle size: size 3–5 (3.25–3.75mm)
Gauge: 23 sts and 32 rows = 4 in (10cm) over knitted St st
Ball size: 126 yd (115m) per 1¾ oz (50g) ball
Yarn specification: 100% cotton

Rowan *Kidsilk Haze*
A fine-weight mohair-blend yarn
Recommended needle size: size 3–8 (3.25–5mm)
Gauge: 18–25 sts and 23–24 rows = 4 in (10cm) over knitted St st
Ball size: 229 yd (210m) per ⅞ oz (25g) ball
Yarn specification: 70% super kid mohair, 30% silk

Rowan *Lurex Shimmer*
A super-fine-weight metallic-mix yarn
Recommended needle size: size 3 (3.25mm)
Gauge: 29 sts and 41 rows = 4 in (10cm) over knitted St st
Ball size: 104 yd (95m) per ⅞ oz (25g) ball
Yarn specification: 80% viscose, 20% polyester

Rowan *RYC Luxury Cotton DK*
A double-knitting weight cotton-blend yarn
Recommended knitting-needle size: size 6 (4mm)
Gauge: 22 sts and 30 rows = 4 in (10cm) over knitted St st
Ball size: 104 yd (95m) per 1¾ oz (50g) ball
Yarn specification: 50% cotton, 45% viscose, 5% silk

Yeoman *Cotton Cannele 4 Ply*
A super-fine-weight mercerized cotton yarn
Recommended needle size: size 2 (2.75mm)
Gauge: 33 sts and 44 rows = 4 in (10cm) over knitted St st
Cone size: 929 yd (875m) per 8¾ oz (250g) cone
Yarn specification: 100% mercerized cotton

abbreviations

beg	begin(ning)
cm	centimeter(s)
cont	continu(e)(ing)
dec	decreas(e)(ing)
garter st	garter stitch (k every row)
foll	follow(s)(ing)
g	gram(s)
inc	increas(e)(ing)
k	knit
m	meter(s)
M1	make one stitch by picking up horizontal loop before next stitch and working into back of it
mm	millimeter(s)
p	purl
patt	pattern; work in pattern
psso	pass slipped stitch over
rep	repeat(ing)
rev St st	reverse stockinette stitch (p all RS rows, k all WS rows)
RS	right side
sl	slip
st(s)	stitch(es)
St st	stockinette stitch (k all RS rows, p all WS rows)
tog	together
WS	wrong side
tbl	through back of loop(s)
yo	yarn over (yarn over right needle to make a new stitch)

[ ] * Repeat instructions between brackets, or after or between asterisks, as many times as instructed.

acknowledgments

My personal thanks and appreciation go to the exceptional people who have collaborated to create this book.

The team at Quadrille Publishing, especially Editorial Director, Jane O'Shea, my mentor, for her constant encouragement and style. Creative Director, Helen Lewis, for her tireless innovation on each new project. Lisa Pendreigh, my wonderful project manager, for her rigorous support and inimitable professionalism.

It has been a privilege to have Katya de Grunwald photograph this book; her exceptional and distinctive work together with stylist Beth Dadswell's unique and inspirational concepts have surpassed my wildest expectations.

My heartfelt thanks to Sally Lee, my brilliant project maker, for her constant support, enthusiasm, expertise, and friendship. And, of course, Rosy Tucker for her inestimable and meticulous hard work in pattern checking.

Stephen Sheard of Coats Craft UK for consistently championing me and Kate Buller, brand manager of Rowan Yarns, and the team for their generosity and enthusiastic support. Also Tony Brooks of Yeoman Yarns for his invaluable assistance.

Finally, this book is dedicated to "creatives" everywhere who continually excite with their passion for the hand made and who push the boundaries of craft by their enthusiasm and innovation. You are my constant source of inspiration.